T0017726

ADHD IS OUR SUPERPOWER

ADHD IS OUR SUPERPOWER

THE AMAZING TALENTS AND SKILLS OF CHILDREN WITH ADHD

Soli Lazarus

Illustrated by Adriana Camargo
Foreword by Daniel Johnson MSP

Jessica Kingsley Publishers
London and Philadelphia

First published in Great Britain in 2021 by Jessica Kingsley Publishers
An Hachette Company

1

Copyright © Soli Lazarus 2021

The right of Soli Lazarus to be identified as the Author of the Work has
been asserted by her in accordance with the Copyright, Designs and
Patents Act 1988.

Front cover illustrations by Adriana Camargo.
Foreword copyright © Daniel Johnson 2021

All rights reserved. No part of this publication may be reproduced,
stored in a retrieval system, or transmitted, in any form or by any
means without the prior written permission of the publisher, nor be
otherwise circulated in any form of binding or cover other than that in
which it is published and without a similar condition being imposed
on the subsequent purchaser.

A CIP catalogue record for this title is available from the British
Library and the Library of Congress

ISBN 978 1 78775 730 1
eISBN 978 1 78775 731 8

Printed and bound in China by Leo Paper Products Ltd

Jessica Kingsley Publishers' policy is to use papers that are natural,
renewable and recyclable products and made from wood grown in
sustainable forests. The logging and manufacturing processes are
expected to conform to the environmental regulations of the
country of origin.

Jessica Kingsley Publishers
Carmelite House
50 Victoria Embankment
London EC4Y 0DZ

www.jkp.com

To Styx who supports me and inspires me every day.
To David and Rosie who make me smile
and make me proud.

Foreword

ADHD can be confusing and bewildering. Whether you are getting to grips with your own diagnosis or helping a child close to you make sense of theirs, it is tricky to understand what ADHD can mean for each individual child. Soli's book takes an important step towards helping children understand what's going on in ADHD brains, why people with ADHD do the things they do and what we can all do to help.

In these pages you will find some simple ways of understanding and working with ADHD. What you will find is that this condition isn't strange and different, but there are strengths and weaknesses that come with it that anyone can relate to.

It also helps to explain that, while it brings challenges, having an ADHD brain can also have its advantages. Being able to hyperfocus, make connections others don't and always seeming to have a creative spark – these are some of the 'superpowers'.

Children with ADHD aren't looking to be treated differently, but what we do need is a bit more understanding. Hopefully this book will help you discuss what this condition means, how to live with it and how to make the most of it. But most of all, I hope this book helps build the understanding of ADHD we all need.

Daniel Johnson, Member of the Scottish Parliament (MSP)

Why I Wrote This Book

Hello, my name is Soli. I am pleased to meet you. Let me tell you a bit about me...

I was a teacher in London primary schools for 30 years and I worked mainly with pupils who found school a bit tricky and difficult. I liked working with these children as I loved their energy and their humour.

My adult son has ADHD and he didn't enjoy school at all. Homelife was also a challenge as there were a lot of arguments. We didn't really know the best way to help him and we got cross with him.

I am really sad about that, as now I know we should have done some things differently.

My job now is to help families who have children with ADHD.

I pass on ideas about what the grown-ups could be doing to make their children happier.

I decided to write this book as I wanted to let all grown-ups know that if you have ADHD it means that you can do amazing things – but you may just need some help and understanding. So, let me introduce you to the girls and boys who have ADHD and also have amazing, incredible superpowers.

I hope you enjoy it.

By the way, my consultancy is called Yellow Sun and I have sneakily included some yellow suns in this book. See if you can find them.

And for the grown-ups, there is a juicy bonus at the end of this book, so don't miss it.

Love, Soli

x

SAM

Hello, my name is Sam and I have ADHD. It stands for Attention Deficit Hyperactivity Disorder.

But I want to tell you that I am not broken, damaged or ill. I have superpowers.

It's a bit complicated but let me try to explain what ADHD is. Inside my skull is my phenomenal brain which acts like a superpowered computer.

My brain sends messages to different parts of my body to do things like feel emotions, talk, stop, move, write, eat, listen, sleep. It's incredible that our brains control our bodies and our emotions, isn't it?

Sometimes the messages get through and everything is okay.

But sometimes the messages don't get through and I may get things wrong. My body is not receiving the messages from my brain. I get into trouble. Grown-ups tell me that I should try harder. But honestly, I am trying as hard as I can.

Grown-ups can help by learning about my ADHD brain and then realizing that I am not being deliberately naughty.

My brain is very busy and is full of thoughts and ideas. Sometimes in life things go wrong. Some people may panic, but my busy brain can come up with some solutions. I'm good to have around when there is a drama! My busy brain is on high alert most of the time.

ADHD is my superpower because when things go wrong, I can keep calm and solve the problem.

ZANE

Hello, my name is Zane and I have ADHD.

I love to move about all the time as it helps me think. You should see me. I am always fidgeting or tapping or sometimes humming.
I am hyperactive as I keep moving, moving, moving.

It makes some grown-ups really irritated and annoyed. If I am told to keep still, it makes me sad and angry. I try very hard to keep still and quiet, but my body works best when I am moving – so I need to have movement breaks. I like doing ten star jumps and afterwards I can focus and concentrate better.

I enjoy jumping on a trampoline, riding my bike and I love to continually bounce a ball. I have so much energy. I take risks, so I often fall over and may hurt myself. It's okay, as so far, I haven't hurt myself too bad.

I also love doodling as it helps me to concentrate. I have made some great patterns with my smelly gel pens, I like the strawberry smell best. My hand just keeps moving! Sometimes I can get really angry if grown-ups don't listen to me when I try to explain what I need. They tell me to keep still, but I can't.

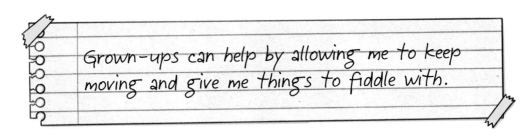

Grown-ups can help by allowing me to keep moving and give me things to fiddle with.

Did you know that the Olympic athletes Simone Biles and Michael Phelps have ADHD? They are using their boundless energy to win gold medals. Yay!

ADHD is my superpower because I have endless energy and I just keep going.

EVA

Hello, my name is Eva and I have ADHD.

I have loads of ideas and I am really imaginative. I love to sing and make up my own songs. I have so many things going on in my brain. Some people call it a 'popcorn brain' as I have so many thoughts going on at the same time. Pop pop pop!

Did you know the singers Zayn Malik and Melanie Brown have ADHD?

Sometimes I look like I am daydreaming because I am thinking about a new idea.

Grown-ups get cross and say I am not listening or paying attention. Sometimes I am thinking about something else when I should be getting ready for school or eating my breakfast.

I try and listen really carefully to what grown-ups are saying to me. Sometimes I hear them but sometimes I just hear 'blah, blah, blah' and I can't concentrate. It may be because I am distracted by a buzzing light, or I may notice a bird outside the window or sometimes it may be because my tummy is rumbling because I didn't finish my breakfast.

Grown-ups can help by kindly reminding me what I need to do or maybe using pictures to help me remember.

I am not being deliberately naughty. I am trying hard, but it's difficult for me to work out what is the important thing I should be doing, or listening to.

I may even be an inventor when I grow up because I think about things that nobody has thought about before.

Some people think that the famous scientist Albert Einstein and the artist Leonardo Da Vinci may have had ADHD.

ADHD is my superpower because I have so many thoughts and creative ideas.

JIM

Hello, my name is Jim and I have ADHD.

My brain is super busy and so I find it hard to remember lots of instructions. Sometimes a grown-up will say things like 'Go upstairs, get dressed, brush your teeth, bring down your book bag and we are leaving in ten minutes'.

Woah! That is far too many things to remember. So I end up doing none of them, and then I get distracted by something else. Grown-ups get really cross with me. It helps when I have a visual schedule to look at so I can easily remember what I need to do.

Grown-ups can help by asking me to do just one thing at a time. Then I would feel successful and we would all be happy.

My busy brain is great when I am planning or thinking of a project I am really interested in. I like to take some risks and know that sometimes these risks can get me into big, big trouble. I can be impulsive, which means I do something before thinking about whether it's a good idea or not. But sometimes the risks I take mean that I find out something interesting.

A lot of famous and successful business people are risk-takers and have ADHD, like Jamie Oliver who is a famous chef and will.i.am who is a very talented music producer.

ADHD is my superpower because I take risks and I am curious which means I may find out new and interesting things.

HEIDI

Hello, my name is Heidi and I have ADHD.

If there are too many things to do, I find it hard to get started.

Sometimes I don't even know what I am meant to be doing, as my busy brain has filled my head with lots and lots of thoughts. I then start to worry that I will get into trouble.

When I am asked to tidy my room, there is so much mess I don't know where to start. So I don't do it, and I get distracted and start playing with my toys instead. Grown-ups shout and sometimes say things like 'Why can't you just listen?!' I am really, really trying to listen, I promise.

It would help if I am asked to do just one thing – like put my socks away. Then it doesn't seem such a massive task and I can get it done.

I also have Dyslexia which is quite common for people with ADHD. This means that I can find reading and writing a bit tricky.

My wrist hurts if I write too much, so I write slowly, but grown-ups sometimes get upset that I haven't done enough, or that my handwriting is messy. It would help if I could use a laptop to write, or a voice recorder to remember what I should be doing.

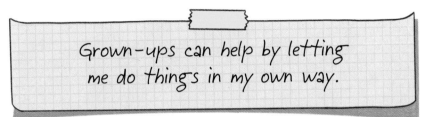

Grown-ups can help by letting me do things in my own way.

Sometimes I think the way I want to do things is much, much better than the way the grown-ups want to do things. I'm good at working out how to solve a problem if I'm really interested in it.

ADHD is my superpower because I am brave and will jump straight into a challenge and give it a go.

VIJAY

Hello, my name is Vijay and I have ADHD.

I love investigating things and grown-ups say I am fearless and I am always trying different things.

But I find it hard to wait my turn, and I interrupt when people are talking. I don't do this deliberately to upset anyone – it's just that I have an idea and I want to share it straight away. I feel I am about to burst, and I can't keep it in. Sometimes I talk really quickly and I might change the subject lots of times.

It would help if I could write down my idea on a whiteboard or a piece of paper.

Putting up my hand and waiting is so hard, it's almost impossible. If the grown-up doesn't ask me for my idea I feel really upset because my idea is a good one.

I also get bored quickly, so it's hard to wait my turn when we are playing a game. Sometimes I say something that hurts people's feelings or is rude. I don't mean it, the words just come tumbling out too quickly.

It makes me feel sad when my friends get cross with me, I am trying my best to be friendly. Sometimes I get left out, sometimes this makes me feel lonely.

My friends tell me I am honest which is a good thing to be, but sometimes I can be impulsive and say things that are honest but may be insensitive.

Grown-ups can help me by suggesting suitable words I could use when I talk to people.
I know I have to try really hard to make and keep friends.

I don't really like playing team sports, but I like things like wall climbing, skating, running, robotics and arts and crafts.

I have a strong sense of what is fair and what is unfair. I notice everything around me, so I can see when I am being treated differently to others, and it can make me cross. It helps when grown-ups ask me my opinion and let me explain. Sometimes the words come out wrong, so please be patient.

ADHD is my superpower because I have a strong sense of what is fair.

CHARLIE

Hello, my name is Charlie and I have ADHD.

I like to feel pressure on my body, so I work best when I am sitting with my back supported or on a wobble cushion. I don't like sitting on the carpet as it makes me feel really dizzy with all that space around me.

I love being hugged, and it makes me feel calm when I have a wobbly feeling in my tummy. I like having a weighted blanket on my bed at night because it makes me feel snuggly and cosy.

It would help if I could sit on a chair, or lie on my tummy on the floor, or stand up. I need to keep moving which sounds strange – but it helps me concentrate.

When I am trying to focus I notice lots of things around me and I get distracted. I notice flickering lights, high-pitch noises, small movements and strong smells. Sometimes these things make me feel uncomfortable and I lose focus and concentration.

Grown-ups can help by understanding that some things make me feel uncomfortable and that they can change their expectation of what I can do.

I am incredibly observant and hypervigilant, so when my sister has lost something tiny, like a sparkly gem, I can find it. I also have really sharp hearing, so I can hear if there's a helicopter coming before anyone else has noticed it. It makes me feel special and unique. I am very curious, and I am aware of things happening around me.

ADHD is my superpower because I notice everything around me.

JASMINE

Hello, my name is Jasmine and I have ADHD.

I have lots of things I am interested in and I love collecting. At the moment I am collecting crystals, but I have also got some great collections of shells and football cards.

But I find it difficult to organize my things. I lose my stuff all the time, I put things down and can't remember where they are. I have to take a lot of equipment to school, and if I leave things to the last minute, I rush around, get in a panic and then I am late. The grown-ups get mad at me.

Actually, I always leave things to the last minute as I think I have plenty of time. Aaargh! But please don't shout at me. That doesn't help.

It helps if I use planners, checklists and alarms to remind me. We have a big whiteboard up on the wall in the kitchen and I look at it to remind me what I need to do.

I like it when the grown-ups notice when I am doing something well, like being kind and helpful. I love it when I find little notes under my pillow. This works better than punishing me. Punishments just make me cross.

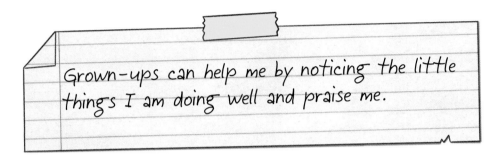

Grown-ups can help me by noticing the little things I am doing well and praise me.

When I am enjoying an activity or looking at something that really interests me, I get animated and excited. I love exploring – when I go outdoors I feel really happy. I love digging and making things with wood.

ADHD is my superpower because I am adventurous.

BOBBY

Hello, my name is Bobby and I have ADHD.

I make lots of people laugh as I have a good sense of humour. I notice the way people talk and behave, and I can mimic them. I have a real eye for detail and notice things that other people miss.

It makes me really happy when people are smiling at me rather than being cross with me.

There are lots of famous comedians, actors and entertainers with ADHD like Rory Bremner, Ant McPartlin, Jim Carrey and Will Smith.

But sometimes I can take a joke too far or make people laugh in class at the wrong time. This gets me into trouble.

I am not deliberately trying to get into trouble – I just thought it was a good idea at the time to make people laugh. I need to learn when it is the right time to be the joker and when to stop.

Sometimes all the things that I am feeling can get too much for me and I cry or scream or get angry. But I know everyone feels these things at some time. Feeling scared, happy, excited, jealous or nervous is all normal. But I go from calm to super angry in a very quick time. It would help me to know the words I can use to describe my emotions and to understand that all emotions are okay.

> Grown-ups can help me to go to a quiet place to calm down.

I use a visual to help me when I feel it's all getting too much. I know my heart starts to race, my hands feel sweaty and my face feels flushed. A grown-up can point to the visual to remind me what I need to do. I have been taught mindfulness exercises and I know some breathing techniques to use as well, like pretending my fingers are candles and blowing them out one at a time. I have made a little den to go to when I feel like I am going to explode. I have a glitter shaker and some headphones and listen to some music. I know that when I feel happier I can talk to a grown-up.

ADHD is my superpower because I am entertaining and can make other people feel happy.

FRANCESCA

Hello, my name is Francesca and I have ADHD.

I love dressing up and making up stories. I have a huge box of dress-up stuff. There are tons of hats and clothes, and my favourite thing is a feather boa. It's so soft and fluffy and tickles my neck, which I like.

But I really don't like going to new places or things like birthday parties or restaurants. There are too many people, too much noise and it makes me feel uncomfortable. I get worried that people won't understand me.

I don't like changing from one thing to another. My body has got used to doing one thing – then I have to change... Gggrrrr.

Grown-ups can help me by using words or pictures to let me know that I am going to be doing something different.

I need time for my body to get used to the new place. We can leave early if I am uncomfortable and getting irritated.

I have a best friend called Fern and we play together at school. We play catch games and search for little stones on the playground. I like being with Fern as she smiles at me and makes me feel happy. Fern likes me because I am honest and I am a good friend.

ADHD is my superpower because I am a caring, lovely person with a warm heart.

ASHER

Hello, my name is Asher and I have ADHD.

I love playing on my Xbox. Minecraft is my totally favourite game. I can focus on it for hours.

Some people wonder why I am not distracted when I am playing an online game.

It's because I am super interested, and it really motivates me. Some people call this hyperfocus. I can focus all my attention on something that extremely motivating for me and I am not distracted by my busy brain.

is

I can hyperfocus on a model I am making or when I am researching about trains. Afterwards though I am very tired because I have put all my energy into concentrating. So grown-ups can help by not asking me to do chores or homework when I am still hyperfocusing on something. This will make me rude and cross.

Instead it would help me if grown-ups let me know gently when it's time to do something else, maybe coming to sit with me, using a timer or a 'now and next' visual aid.

I get bored really quickly. If I am not really interested in the thing I am doing, I get distracted and feel restless, I lose focus. So if things are fun and engaging, I can concentrate more.

Grown-ups can help by letting us decide together what the rules will be, and that the rules are fair.

I also like going on my Xbox because I am good at it and no one complains when I get things wrong. I also like talking to my friends online and no one criticizes me. I know I must listen to the grown-ups about being safe online and only watching things that are okay for my age.

ADHD is my superpower because when I hyperfocus I can get a lot done.

SARITA

Hello, my name is Sarita and I have ADHD.

I have a little sister called Olivia. Olivia doesn't have ADHD. Sometimes I get jealous of Olivia because she doesn't get into trouble like I do. She can sit at the table without fidgeting and she can get her work done with no problems.

Sometimes I don't like Olivia, but I don't mean to be nasty. I may push her, but I do it without thinking first. I love Olivia but I am jealous that the grown-ups treat her differently. This makes me cry but also makes me cross. Sometimes my emotions get too much and I get really, really cross. Sometimes Olivia tries to get me into trouble by telling tales to the grown-ups.

Punishments don't work because I am not being deliberately unkind to Olivia. If I get sent to my room as a punishment it just makes me really angry and sad.

> Grown-ups can help by explaining my ADHD to other members of my family.

It's great when we all play together and have fun. When we are laughing I forget that I am cross. I also like it when a grown-up spends special time just with me.

At school I am happy when the teachers ask me to help the younger children at lunchtime. It makes me feel special and important.

I like it when I am asked to help Olivia with something she cannot do. It makes me feel proud that I am her clever big sister.

ADHD is my superpower because I am great at helping younger children.

LAINI

Hello, my name is Laini
and I have ADHD.

And guess what?
My mum has ADHD too.
She also finds some things
difficult, so we work them
out together.

If I eat a healthy diet and exercise it helps my focus and concentration. I take special pills from the doctor that help the messages reach the correct part of my brain. Clever isn't it?

Sometimes I cannot sleep. It helps if I have a routine at night-time and calm activities before bed. I like sleeping with a buzzing fan or gentle music as it stops my busy brain thinking about things. I make sure my phone is charging downstairs overnight, so I am not distracted... Zzzzzzz.

Sometimes I get a bit worried or anxious as I miss instructions, I may get things wrong and I can see I upset people. I am trying my best. When I worry my tummy feels tight and sometimes I get a headache.

I have a worry box that I use when something is upsetting me. I write little notes on a Post-it and put it in the box. A grown-up can read the note and talk to me about how I am feeling. This helps me to stop worrying.

Grown-ups can help by finding out what food I can eat that will help me concentrate better.

One thing I love to do is make and design my own clothes. I customize shoes, t-shirts and bags. Everyone says they are really special and unique. Just like me!

ADHD is my superpower because it makes me who I am. I am me.

ADHD IS OUR SUPERPOWER

We have ADHD and it is our superpower. And we are amazing!

We want the grown-ups to understand that we are not being deliberately naughty, difficult or rude.

We are trying our best. But our brains behave in a different way that makes it hard for us to focus, concentrate and to keep still.

We know we interrupt, we can be quite forgetful and try risky things. But we are not bad or broken.

We have amazing talents and skills, and if grown-ups give us a chance and help us, we know we can be really successful and live incredible and happy lives.

Please show us kindness.

Lots of love,

Sam, Zane, Eva, Jim, Heidi, Vijay, Charlie, Jasmine, Bobby, Francesca, Asher, Sarita and Laini

ADHD Is Your Superpower

Now you've met the ADHD gang, you've seen that each one has superpowers. The girls and boys in this book may be similar to you. You may fiddle, forget things or have a busy brain that makes it difficult to sleep.

So I bet you also have superpowers.

Do you love a challenge? Do you have great ideas? Do you notice things around you that other people don't see? Are you able to hyperfocus on something and so can get a lot done?

It's great to have ADHD and to have these superpowers. It means that you can lead a really happy and successful life.

You can choose whatever you want to be.

There are many grown-ups with ADHD who are teachers, doctors, actors, journalists, police officers, MPs and inventors. You may know someone in your family who has ADHD and they may run a successful business.

These grown-ups live happy lives. You can too.

PEOPLE WHO CAN HELP YOU

The doctor
If the grown-ups think you may have ADHD, then you can go to see your doctor. Your name will then go on a waiting list for you to see an ADHD specialist who will decide if you have ADHD.

ADHD specialist
You will be asked lots of questions and the specialist will ask your parents lots of questions. Your teachers will also fill in a form. Then the specialist will decide if you have ADHD. Your parents may also be tested to see if they have ADHD as the specialists know that ADHD is highly genetic and runs in families.

Medication
Some children take medication prescribed by the specialist. These pills can help an ADHD brain to send messages and signals to the body to help with emotions, focus and concentration. Not all children with ADHD take medication.

Family support
Sometimes parents are offered support by a professional who can help the whole family. This person will give advice

about how things in the home could be different, so that you can all get on better and be happier. Grown-ups can contact me for more information as I would love to help your family. Here is my email address: soli@yellow-sun.com

Support for you
You may feel like talking to a grown-up about your ADHD. Your parents will help you find someone you can trust. This could be someone in your family, someone at school or a professional who understands that ADHD is part of who you are (and you are amazing!).

CO-MORBID CONDITIONS

Children with ADHD are likely to have another condition as well. These are called co-morbid conditions, and could be Dyslexia, Dyspraxia, Dyscalculia or Autism. These conditions all come under the same neurodiversity label and many clever scientists think that all the conditions are linked. This is good news as it means that if you have been diagnosed with ADHD, grown-ups can be on the lookout for other things you find difficult and find things to help you.

How Grown-Ups Can Help You

HERE IS A LIST OF THINGS THAT GROWN-UPS CAN DO THAT MAY HELP YOU AT HOME

There are spaces so the grown-ups can add their own ideas.

- ☐ put up visual lists and pictures to remind you what to do

- ☐ put together a schedule or planner so you know what is happening

- ☐ help you with organizing your stuff using things like colour-coded folders and drawers

- ☐ set timers so you can see how long is left

- ☐ ask your opinion and listen to your ideas

- ☐ set up a calm area you can go to if you feel it's all too much

- [ ] use images to help you understand emotions
- [ ] ask you to do just one thing at a time
- [ ] come up with lots of fun things for you to try
- [ ] provide plenty of opportunities to use up your energy
- [ ] have realistic expectations of things you can do
- [ ] keep praising and noticing the little things you do well
- [ ] not compare you to your siblings
- [ ] role model how to communicate with your siblings
- [ ] give you opportunities to be successful
- [ ] decide rules with you
- [ ] see if you have any sensory needs or difficulties
- [ ] provide you with a healthy diet that is high protein and low sugar
- [ ] set up a calm bedtime routine
- [ ] help you create a worry box or book if you need it
- [ ] educate the whole family about ADHD
- [ ] ....
- [ ] ....
- [ ] ....
- [ ] ....

HERE IS A LIST OF THINGS THAT GROWN-UPS CAN DO THAT MAY HELP YOU AT SCHOOL

There are spaces so the grown-ups can add their own ideas.

☐ attend ADHD training

☐ set up regular meetings with your parents

☐ request a one-page document showing what helps you and what doesn't help you

☐ present work to be done in small steps

☐ use a lot of visuals so you understand what you need to do

☐ use a timer so you know how long is left

☐ ask for your opinion and listen to your ideas

☐ provide equipment that will help you, such as sensory, laptop or visual aids

☐ make sure there are few sensory distractions in the classroom

☐ set up an area of the classroom where you can work if you want to and won't be distracted

☐ provide a whiteboard for you to write down your ideas, answer a question or to doodle on

- [ ] select pupils to answer a question using random selectors such as lolly sticks (which is fairer than hands up)

- [ ] allow you to have water and movement breaks

- [ ] role model how to communicate with your classmates

- [ ] celebrate your achievements and the things you can do well

- [ ] use visual images to help you understand emotions

- [ ] set up a calm area you can go to if you feel it's all too much

- [ ] make homework easy enough for you to do quickly and on your own

- [ ] use a reward system that is not on public display (personal rewards are great)

- [ ] understand that punishments do not work (what does work is kindness and the understanding that your brain works differently)

- [ ] ....

- [ ] ....

- [ ] ....

- [ ] ....

JUICY BONUS

I have produced some free bonus material that provide
a more detailed explanation of the subjects featured in
this book:

- Features of ADHD

- Sensory Sensitivities

- Executive Function Difficulties

- Co-Morbid Conditions

- Emotional Overwhelm

- Rewards + Punishments

- Raising Self-Esteem

- Organization

- Sleep

- Diet

- Strategies for School

Check it out at: www.adhd-superpowers.com

BOOKS FOR GROWN-UPS THAT SOLI LOVES

The Explosive Child, Fifth Edition: A New Approach for Understanding and Parenting Easily Frustrated, Chronically Inflexible Children by Ross Greene (Harper Paperbacks, 2014).

What Your ADHD Child Wishes You Knew: Working Together to Empower Kids for Success in School and Life by Dr Sharon Saline (Tarcherperigee, 2018).

The Spectrum Girl's Survival Guide: How to Grow Up Awesome and Autistic by Siena Castellon (Jessica Kingsley Publishers, 2020).

Boy Without Instructions: Surviving the Learning Curve of Parenting a Child with ADHD by Penny Williams (Grace-Everett Press, 2014).

Driven to Distraction: Recognizing and Coping with Attention Deficit Disorder from Childhood Through Adulthood by Ned Halliwell (Touchstone, 1995).

Sulky, Rowdy, Rude?: Why Kids Really Act Out and What to Do About It by Bo Hejlskov Elven and Tina Wiman (Jessica Kingsley Publishers, 2017).

How to Talk So Kids Will Listen and Listen So Kids Will Talk by Adele Faber and Elaine Mazlish (Piccadilly Press, 2013).

Get Out My Life. But First Take Me and Alex into Town by Tony Wolf and Suzanne Franks (Profile Books, 2014).

USEFUL WEBSITES

www.addiss.co.uk
The national UK information and support service for families and adults with ADHD with 25 years of experience. It also has a national helpline and can refer families to appropriate local services and organizations.

www.adhdaction.org
A UK charity working to bring about change in understanding and assessing ADHD. One of their aims is to establish an ADHD Act to enable a statutory set of guidelines in Education, the Health Sector and the Prison Service.

www.adhdfoundation.org.uk
A UK charity providing a wealth of resources and training to enable those with ADHD to improve their life chances.

www.additudemag.com
A US online publication that produces a vast library of up-to-date advice and information on ADHD.

www.specialneedsjungle.com
A UK parent-led information board for parents of young people with special needs.

www.sossen.org.uk
A UK charity offering free legal, education, health and care plan (EHCP) and statutory rights advice on special needs.

www.qlmentoring.com

Peer mentoring for bright kids with Autism and learning differences, including Dyslexia, Dyspraxia and Sensory Processing Disorder.

HOW I CAN HELP YOU

- 1:1 Bespoke Family Support
- Together Stronger Club. An online membership for coaching and training
- Monthly Support Group
- Online ADHD Course
- Teacher Training in Schools
- Talk to Parent Groups and Charities

All details and information on my website: www.soli-lazarus.com

Contact me at: soli@yellow-sun.com

About Us

SOLI LAZARUS B.EDUC (PSYCHOLOGY)

Soli means 'sunshine' in French, so that is why I chose 'Yellow Sun' as my consultancy name, which I set up to support families and young people who have ADHD. I am a former teacher with 30 years' experience and was a special educational needs coordinator (SENCO) at a large primary school in London. My adult son has ADHD and so I know what it is like to struggle and feel isolated, whilst also loving the joy and unpredictability  of my beautiful son. I am a public speaker to parent groups and charities, and train teachers nationwide in the UK. I write a regular blog, produce a podcast and have a thriving Facebook group.

I help families through bespoke 1:1 support as well as running an interactive, caring online membership. I'm passionate about busting the stigma around ADHD and attend the All-Party Parliamentary Group on ADHD in UK Parliament. I am also a Trustee of the UK charity ADHD Action. Finally, I love my family, singing, dancing, painting, gardening, being outdoors, Tottenham Hotspur Football Club, Robbie Williams and all things yellow!

Contact: soli@yellow-sun.com

ABOUT ADRIANA CAMARGO

Adriana is an illustrator and graphic designer from Colombia. Her great curiosity has led her to explore different techniques to adapt her drawings and characters to 2D, 3D and even ceramic formats; she has published board games and even illustrated this book for you.

Contact: adriana.camargo.kf@gmail.com